Up and Down

Eric James

INFOMAX COMMON CORE READERS

Rosen Classroom™

New York

Published in 2013 by The Rosen Publishing Group, Inc.
29 East 21st Street, New York, NY 10010

Book Design: Michael Harmon

Photo Credits: Cover © iStockphoto.com/knape; p. 5 p. Stelian Ion/Shutterstock.com; p. 7 Darryl West/Shutterstock.com; p. 9 Anastasija Popova/Shutterstock.com; p. 11 © iStockphoto.com/konradlew; p. 13 Warren Goldswain/Shutterstock.com; p. 15 Alex James Bramwell/Shutterstock.com.

ISBN: 978-1-4488-8878-8
6-pack ISBN: 978-1-4488-8879-5

Manufactured in the United States of America

CPSIA Compliance Information: Batch #WS12RC: For further information contact Rosen Publishing, New York, New York at 1-800-237-9932.

Word Count: 24

Contents

The bird is up.

The bird is down.

The cat is up.

The cat is down.

The ball is up.

The ball is down.

Words to Know

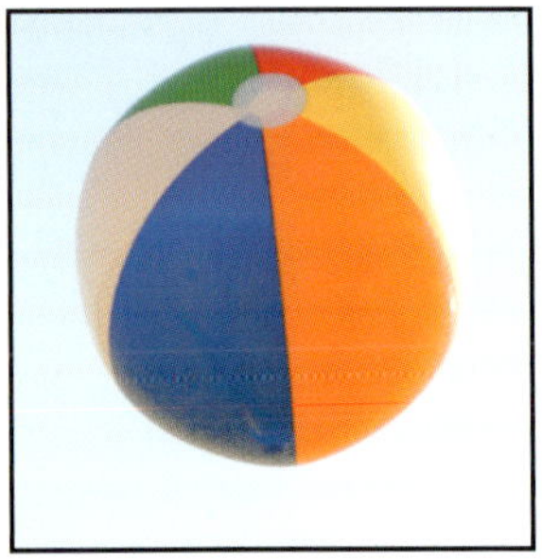

ball

bird

cat

Index